WAR ON SICKNESS

Brenda Kunneman

www.TotalPublishingAndMedia.com

War On Sickness
© 2023 by Brenda Kunneman

Published by: 3Dream Studios in association with Total Publishing and
Media, LLC

3Dream Studios, LLC
7711 E 111ᵗʰ St.
Suite 125
Tulsa, OK 74133
(918) 394-7711

Total Publishing And Media
5411 South 125th East Ave.
Suite 302
Tulsa, OK 74146
(918) 624-9300

Unless otherwise noted, Scripture quotations are taken from the New King
James Version®. Copyright © 1982 by Thomas Nelson. Used by permission.
All rights reserved.

Scripture quotations marked NLT are taken from the Holy Bible, New Living
Translation, © 1996, 2004. Used by permission of Tyndale House Publishers,
Inc., Carol Stream, Illinois 60188. All rights reserved.

Paperback ISBN: 978-1-63302-277-5
E-Book ISBN: 978-1-63302-278-2

Printed in the United States of America

TABLE OF CONTENTS

CHAPTER 1

IT'S A WAR

We as a Church must take back our right to stand in divine health. As a body, believers have been under attack as never before. I believe that COVID-19 was an all-out, direct demonic attack against our faith, aimed at the Church to chip away at our assurance in the promises of God. The enemy sought to shake our trust in God's healing, His provision, and His faithfulness.

The question is: Will we let the enemy shake our faith?

I hope you know this, but we are in a *war*, and our enemy seeks to keep us from walking in healing. The devil knows that we can believe God's promises to be true without actually walking in them and that there are blessings in the Bible that some Christians will never attain. Why? Because we have allowed fear and disbelief to scare us and shake our faith in God.

That's why it is time for the Church to rise up, seize the promises God has given to us, and fight back with the spiritual weapons of our warfare against the tide of fear and disease under which the enemy desires to crush us.

We, as a body, have gotten weak about divine healing, including the charismatic Church. You can tell by the way you hear people talking about and glorifying negative things—the conditions, the aches and pains, the diseases. The way we have been using our words has been diminishing our covenant right, a promise God has given His people, to be *healed*.

But, thank Jesus, God is not going to leave us under attack by the enemy with no recourse! In fact, it is just the opposite. The Holy Spirit wants to build and restore our faith, raise us up, and refresh our trust in the God who heals us, the very One who *died* for our healing, taking the stripes upon His back so that we could be made whole. This is a war, and the Lord of Heaven's Armies is calling us to stand up and kick the devil in the teeth, to take hold of the promises God has given us, and to stand firm against the powers of evil that are trying to afflict the Church!

We don't have to be sick just because the world is sick. We've allowed the enemy to bring the same fear upon us as he has the rest of the world. Christians are first in line, whipped up by fear, to get a vaccine that may or may not work; terrified of what may happen if we gather together; and trust in masks that can't stop a tiny virus more than we trust the living God. That isn't God's plan for us!

We don't have to be subject to the same afflictions and diseases of this world, like COVID, cancer, or anything else, because the Lord has *always* made provision for His people! We are going to look at many of the promises God has given us to stand upon to show us beyond doubt that it's His will to heal us, that He never changes, and that you can trust God's will to heal and power to do so, even in an era of pandemics and rampant fear.

The Church is not to cower in fear before the enemy! We're supposed to storm his gates—because we know that our enemy's greatest strongholds cannot stand before us! No matter the condition, from COVID to heart disease, cancer to diabetes, it is not God's will for *any* of His people to be sick and afflicted by the devil. Together over the next few chapters, we're going to see God's plan and provision.

It is my prayer that in reading this small book, God is going to build your faith. I prophesy over you and come into agreement with you that you will rise up in our covenant with God to take hold of the victory He offers, to say "No!" to the devil, and to say "Yes and Amen!" to all of God's promises. If Jesus paid for our healing, then we ought to be able to walk in it. If He took our diseases, then those diseases are not ours anymore. Divine wholeness and healing are yours and mine, and we don't have to just quietly sit and take things from the devil when we can instead have the amazing and powerful gifts of God that Jesus died and rose again to provide for us.

If that sounds good, if you want God to restore your faith, build you up with His promises, and heal you and set you free, you've picked up the right book! Get ready, because that is exactly what God is going to do, for you and for those for whom you pray, because the enemy has been getting victories in the war on sickness long enough.

It's time to take back the territory he stole, because the Lord always causes the thief to repay what he's taken.

Are you ready to get your healing back? Then let's dive into the Word of God, because the fact is that we stand on one incredible truth that precedes all others: it is God's will for us to be healed. I can't wait to show you the message God has given me for His people—for *you*—because He always wants to heal you! The war against sickness isn't over; no, despite all the things the enemy has tried to do, overwhelming victory is ours through Christ. So if you are hungry for divine healing, get ready to shout, because God is empowering the Church to take the war on sickness to the devil—and he'd better look out, because the gates of hell cannot stand before us!

CHAPTER 2

IT'S GOD'S WILL FOR YOU TO BE HEALED

In the previous chapter, I told you that I believe we are in a war against sickness. Events in our world and just the constant wear and tear of life have broken people down and worn out so many of God's children. Yet, we do not need to settle for the same afflictions as the world. Instead, we can walk in divine healing, and in this chapter we're going to look at just a handful of the Scriptures that show us how God feels about healing and reveal His heart.

Many people know it in theory, but fewer stand on this promise firmly—it is *always* God's will for us to be healed. Some have never heard this, and others quickly think of a reason to doubt that statement because of an experience they feel disproves it.

For the first group, you may have grown up under a Church that doesn't think the gifts of the Spirit are for today and taught that things such as miracles and healings passed away with the Early Church. Countless people are in this category, and I too went to school with those who believed this way, but God showed me in His Word that the truth is the gifts of God are without repentance—they're irrevocable and can never be withdrawn—and they don't change because *He* doesn't change. God is still the Healer and is still in the healing business!

For the others, those who have perhaps lost someone, who have prayed but didn't get the healing, or who have doubts, the Lord wants to build up your faith afresh. He wants to show you His heart as the healer in a supernatural way that it will dispel any doubts that have arisen through life's difficult circumstances. It is my prayer that as you read this book, God is going to reset your heart with a fresh and innocent faith again.

In the course of this book, we're going to look at the conditions for being healed, according to the Word. We're also going to see the role our faith plays and how incredibly important our words are. But before we dive into that, I believe the most important point God wants to build up within you is first about Him, not us.

It is *always* God's will for you to be healed.

Right off the bat, I know this is going to throw some people off. Those who have been taught incorrect doctrine and those who have prayed but did not see the healing will question it. That is why I urge you to set aside whatever you think you know or have experienced to get a divine reset and fresh take, not from my opinions but from what God says in the Bible.

Starting with the Old Testament, we're going to walk through some of the most powerful healing Scriptures. You can find a list of healing scriptures starting on page 75 of this book. I love that the Bible is on our devices, but if you're anything like me, you're easily distracted by your phone. I'll be trying to pay attention to the things of God, but it's like my phone knows how to distract me. Since few of us ever really turn off those interrupting notifications, I really like the idea of having God's promises on a piece of paper that you can tape up somewhere or carry with you. They're for you in the back of this book, but for right now, let's dive into the Word and see God's heart as the Healer.

The Lord Who Heals You

The first thing God wants you to see is that He has *always* made healing provision for His people, even under the Old Covenant. There was no sickness in the Garden of Eden before the fall; we were not created to get sick and die. Death and disease entered the world with sin.

Our first Scripture comes at a time when God's people were oppressed and overworked in captivity to the Egyptians. They needed to know God's will toward them, and we read it in a powerful verse in Exodus 15:26:

> *If you diligently heed the voice of the Lord your God and do what is right in His sight, give ear to His commandments and keep all His statutes, I will put none of the diseases on you which I have brought on the Egyptians. For I am the Lord who heals you.*

7

The first part of this verse describes one of the conditions I mentioned earlier and that we'll cover in detail in future chapters, but that's not what I want you to focus on right now. Key in on the last sentence of this Scripture, because God is telling us who He is—*the Lord who heals us.*

I want you to notice something else from this passage that's very important. God tells them that He will not put any of the diseases on His people that He put on the Egyptians. This is backed up in Deuteronomy 7:15, which says, *"And the Lord will take away from you all sickness, and will afflict you with none of the terrible diseases of Egypt which you have known, but will lay them on all those who hate you."* Go back and read that again. How much sickness? *Some* of it? No, the promise is that He will take away *all* sickness from His people.

Sickness and disease came with the curse, but I am so thankful to be part of the family of God! We are not subject to the curse, and when God brought the plagues on the Egyptians, we read that those things did not afflict the land of Goshen where God's people lived in captivity. While the world may experience the curse, we as children of God are not subject to those things. God has always held His people apart, and that will never change.

God held this up even in the greatest of the plagues, where the angel of death moved throughout Egypt. In the land of Goshen, the people marked their doorposts with blood, and the angel passed over. God gave His people this promise: *"So you shall serve the Lord your God, and He will bless your bread and your water. And I will take sickness away from the midst of you"* (Exodus 23:25).

This is an incredibly comforting verse to me, because this tells me not only do we have the promise that God will take sickness from the midst of our lives, but He is going to bless our provision as well! Just as we have no need to fear the sickness and disease that is in the world, we also have no fear of downturns in the economy or inflation. Stores may run out of something like chicken, but God has promised to provide. If you are meant to eat chicken, God will provide it, so have confidence that when you need it, God will provide it. The same God who provides all you need also is the One who heals you!

The people who say healing is not for today might as well chop these passages out of their Bibles! But I don't serve the God of former promises or who He was yesterday; I serve the God who is the same yesterday, today, and forever (Hebrews 13:8)! And if He tells me that He is the Lord who heals me, and He tells me He will bless my bread and water and take sickness away, I believe Him!

Do you? If you're still struggling, take heart—God is going to rebuild that faith. Faith comes by hearing the Word of God, and we're far from done, dear reader.

Since we've been looking at a couple of passages from Exodus, I want to give you one more verse from that period in the life of God's people that I find very powerful. Psalms tells us something about these people as they received God's promises: not only did God call them out of Egypt and ensure they had bread and water, He sent the wealth of Egypt with them! We read, "*He also brought them out with silver and gold, and there was none feeble among His tribes*" (Psalms 105:37). This means they were walking in

God's promise—right out of Egypt and into God's strength! They were loaded with the silver and gold of the world, and they did not stumble or falter, because there was no sickness among them.

A few chapters later, Psalm 107:20 says, *"He sent His word and healed them, and delivered them from their destructions."* One translation ends that verse by saying, *"snatching them from the door of death"* (NLT).

So what was the Word sent to do? *Heal us!*

I hope that, like me, you're taking in these healing promises. However, this is just a smattering of passages from the Old Testament. We haven't even looked at the Scriptures surrounding Jesus' ministry and all the times He healed, but take a moment to think on this: John tells us that Jesus was the Word made flesh, and here in Psalms God is telling us that God sent His Word and healed us. Do you see the heart of the Father here? Hundreds of years before Jesus was born, God had already given Him His marching orders—to heal—and then sent Him to earth to accomplish that and so much more. Let's quickly take a look at some prophecies about Jesus' earthly ministry.

Surely

Jesus fulfilled hundreds of prophecies during His earthly ministry, but some of the most powerful regarding our healing. Hundreds of years before He was born, Isaiah 53:4-5 prophesied,

> *Surely He has borne our griefs and carried our sorrows; yet we esteemed Him stricken, smitten by*

God, and afflicted. But He was wounded for our transgressions, He was bruised for our iniquities; the chastisement for our peace was upon Him, and by His stripes we are healed.

When you see the word "surely," you know it to be true. If I told you that surely I was going to give you $100, do you expect to get the money? Yes, because I didn't say "maybe" I'll give it to you or "possibly." I told you *surely*—you can be sure of it. When God gives you a promise, you can take it to the bank!

Let's go back and look at this passage in more detail, because I want you to understand a few of these words could be translated differently. When it says "griefs" here, that can also be translated as "sicknesses," and the word for "sorrows" can be rendered as "pains." This passage is laying out that Jesus carried our sicknesses and even our pains. If you're reading this, and something hurts in your body right now, read that passage again for yourself—*"Surely* He has borne *your* sicknesses and carried *your* pains."

Everything our sin deserves, Jesus took on Himself. He was stricken and afflicted, not randomly or because the Romans decided to, but because it was part of fulfilling promises just like this one. So many readily accept that Jesus died for our sins and that we have salvation through the finished work of the cross, but some people forget that as He was paying for our sins, He was also paying the price for our healing!

"*By His stripes we are healed,*" the Bible tells us. Not "might be" healed, or "if God's in a good mood" we'll be healed. By His stripes, we *are* healed!

I mentioned that, as a young woman, I went to a school that didn't believe in healing, and they would tell me this passage meant emotional healing or spiritual healing only. Yet, this Scripture specifies that He was wounded for our transgressions and was bruised for our iniquities—our sins. Yet, then it clearly says that the physical stripes on His back paid for our healing!

Jeremiah 30:17 gives us another wonderful promise: "*'For I will restore health to you and heal you of your wounds,'says the Lord.*" Every word in the Bible is important, so read that again carefully and see the words "I will." What is God's will, according to the Bible? This very verse tells you God's will is to heal!

I could go on regarding this for some time, but I want to cover some amazing passages about Jesus' earthly ministry prophesied hundreds of years before His birth before we look at some New Testament promises in the next chapter.

One of these is a personal favorite: "*But to you who fear My name the Sun of Righteousness shall arise with healing in His wings; and you shall go out and grow fat like stall-fed calves*" (Malachi 4:2). I love this promise, but also see that God lays out a condition: this is a promise to those who fear His name.

These Scriptures paint a picture of a God who loves to heal His people. He does not heal us grudgingly; He does so as a loving Father. I have given you just a handful of

Scriptures, all pointing to the fact that God's will is to heal His people!

The entire Old Testament is a type and shadow of promises Jesus fulfilled, symbolism rich with meaning and pointing to the Way, the Truth, and the Life—Jesus Christ, the Sun of Righteousness who rose from the dead with healing in His wings. On earth, Jesus did nothing on His own, only doing what He saw the Father doing. With this understanding of how the Old Testament points the way to a healing Jesus, who revealed the heart of the Father, let's look at the New Testament at these promises fulfilled in the next chapter.

CHAPTER 3

HE HEALED THEM ALL

Let's be honest, when we read the Bible, we see that many Christians do not live according to the promises of the Word. All too often, we do not experience God's will, which is to heal us; instead, the Church often finds itself suffering the same afflictions as the world. This should not be so! As we saw in the previous chapter, when it comes to divine healing, the Bible shows us a God who wants to bless us, who wants to deliver us, who wants to heal His people.

God made this provision for Israel, and in the wilderness not only were there no feeble ones among them, but their shoes didn't even wear out! If you tried to push the Church through the Red Sea today, I sometimes wonder if we would make it, with all of our weakness, sickness, pains, and complaining.

Yet as we've seen, long before Jesus walked the earth in a physical body, God made sure that His people were well taken care of and showed us His heart to heal. So why are we, the New Testament Church, not walking more in this power? If we're sick and exhausted, how will we preach the Gospel where it needs to be preached? How will we reach those who have not heard, and how will they see the difference between God's people and the world? This isn't the path of healing Jesus demonstrated to us, so we need a change.

You don't have to read very far into the four Gospels to see some of the countless stories of how Jesus healed the sick during His earthly ministry. It is vital to understand the fact that for all the healings that Jesus did throughout Scripture, He was not acting on His own. Jesus came to do His Father's will, and everything He did exemplified God's heart. Jesus walked this earth as the deliverer, the giver of blessings, the forgiver of sins, and the Healer. In fact, He went around healing *all* who were oppressed by the devil.

I want to share with you one of my favorite passages about Jesus, because it encapsulates so much. In Matthew 8:16-17 we read,

> *When evening had come, they brought to Him many who were demon-possessed. And He cast out the spirits with a word, and healed all who were sick, that it might be fulfilled which was spoken by Isaiah the prophet, saying: 'He Himself took our infirmities and bore our sicknesses.'*

How many did He heal and deliver? *All* who were sick. And what was the result? Jesus was fulfilling the prophecies about Him being our Healer! By being who He was and doing what the Father sent Him to do, Jesus went around fulfilling every prophecy as a matter of course. And all of it revealed the heart of the Father.

Did Jesus just heal the ones He liked? The ones who asked nicely? Maybe He only healed the ones who knew all the religious things to say? No, He healed *all of them.* Why? Because they were God's children, oppressed by sickness and Satan, and this shows that God's will is for all His children to be healed and set free!

If we were in a church service together and I took your Bible, who has the Bible? I would have it, because I took it. If I took it, you don't have it anymore, right? I know this sounds overly simplistic, but you need to understand that if Jesus took our infirmities and bore our sicknesses on the cross, *we don't have them anymore!* We readily believe He took our sins, but the Word clearly states that He bore our sins and our infirmities.

Do we believe it?

If you believe that Jesus took stripes for your healing, I want you to do something as an act of faith. Take your hand and place it over your heart and say with me, "Jesus took sickness off of my body, off of my mind, out of my blood, and from my heart." If you need healing in a part of your body, say that part out loud right now in prayer, affirming the Word of God that Jesus *already* paid the price and already took those things upon Himself.

When He died, your sins and mine went to the grave with Him. But they did not rise again with Him! They went down, but they didn't come up!

God's will from start to finish has been healing for His people. All four Gospels are packed full of stories about Jesus encountering people who were sick and oppressed by the devil and healing them and setting them free. From blindness to deafness to paralysis to even death itself, none of it could stand before Him! He didn't debate it, think about it, or spend time in prayer wondering if it was God's will to heal; He simply did it!

I love passages like this next one, which happens right after Jesus walks on water before they arrived at Gennesaret, where He'd set a man free who was oppressed by a legion of demons. *"And when the men of that place recognized Him, they sent out into all that surrounding region, brought to Him all who were sick, and begged Him that they might only touch the hem of His garment. And as many as touched it were made perfectly well"* (Matthew 14:35-36). We read a similar one in Matthew 4:23: *"And Jesus went about all Galilee, teaching in their synagogues, preaching the gospel of the kingdom, and healing all kinds of sickness and all kinds of disease among the people."*

I want you to see here that healing was not a difficult thing to get from Jesus. He did not hand it out sparingly, and they did not have to struggle or strive or fight to get it. Like a loving parent giving good gifts to His children, Jesus showed that the heart of the Father is to heal His people!

Jesus also didn't heal people so He could simply prove that He was the Son of God. Many have tried to assert this as the reason, but this line of thinking cannot be supported by the fact that God *always* made a healing provision for His people, prior to Jesus' ministry! Sure, Jesus' healing power reflected His deity, but that wasn't the reason He healed people. He healed people because God loves them and to show God's heart as the Healer! Otherwise, He would not have borne our sicknesses and taken away our diseases. To demonstrate the Kingdom and show God's heart for healing and His will to heal *you*, Jesus healed all manner of sicknesses and all manner of diseases among God's people because that's who He is! I urge you, read the Gospels and note every time Jesus healed—and all the times it says He healed them *all*! I wish there were more time to list all His healings, but we need to shift gears to see that healing did not end with Jesus.

Healing Is the Standard

Healing is the standard of the Kingdom of God, and that's why when Jesus sent out His disciples, He gave them authority to cast out demons and heal the sick. They, too, were to show what God was like, and just as Jesus commissioned His disciples to cast down devils and raise up healing, Jesus empowered the Early Church in the Book of Acts with the Holy Spirit so that we could do the same! And nothing has changed since then; we still have the Holy Spirit's power just as surely as they did, and that means that it is our mission, also, to heal the sick and cast out the devil.

After receiving power in the Upper Room, the Early Church followed Jesus' same pattern of healing, showing that this did not end with Him. One of the best illustrations of this is when Peter and John went to the temple to pray and saw a lame man by the temple gate called Beautiful. Peter got his attention, and the man got excited about receiving something from them—it just wasn't what he thought it was going to be!

> *Then Peter said, 'Silver and gold I do not have, but what I do have I give you: In the name of Jesus Christ of Nazareth, rise up and walk.' And he took him by the right hand and lifted him up, and immediately his feet and ankle bones received strength. So he, leaping up, stood and walked and entered the temple with them—walking, leaping, and praising God. And all the people saw him walking and praising God.*
>
> Acts 3:6-9

We could go on and on with examples after Jesus ascended to heaven, and despite what certain denominations incorrectly teach, these gifts did not pass away at some vague time in the Early Church. The Holy Spirit didn't lose effectiveness or get old in the past 2,000 years. The Holy Spirit is alive and well today in the Church, healing and setting people free from the enemy!

You cannot tell me that it is not God's will to heal. There's too much in the Word describing His heart, and I have seen His power demonstrated too many times to believe God has anything else in His heart for us but healing. God has always wanted his people well, and Jesus made provision for our healing by taking stripes on His back, then rising again with healing in His wings.

Put your hand on your heart again and declare, "Healing is mine because Jesus paid for it! God wants me well, able to accomplish every purpose He put me on this earth to do. I take authority over sickness, disease, pain, and suffering, and I declare war on them in the power and authority of Jesus' name! They must go! I draw a line in the sand against the enemy. He is a liar, and he must get off my body, out of my family, and away from my purpose! In the authority of Jesus' name, I am the healed of the Lord, and as of this moment I begin walking in the healing Jesus bought and paid for!"

If Jesus took our sickness, then it's *gone*. Anything else is a lie, because it has no right to stay on you. Jesus took stripes for your healing, and walking in it is your divine right as a blood-bought child of the living God! The devil may have gotten by with putting sickness on you in the past, but it's time to retake the territory he has stolen. The Bible shows us God's heart is to heal, and Jesus demonstrated that fully as He walked the earth. But then He left us His Holy Spirit, the Spirit of power, as well as the authority of Jesus' name that we would never again be subject to the sickness and death of this world. They're defeated foes, and this battle we are in is not to win the war—it's to enforce the victory Jesus already won!

In the next few chapters, I want to open the Word together and show you the pathways God gives us for walking in healing throughout the Bible. These are not hoops to jump through, and not all of them are unique to healing. If you want to consistently walk in divine healing, I believe God has a battle plan for His people that will allow us to take this fight against sickness to the enemy—and experience God's victory over sickness!

CHAPTER 4

GOD'S PATH TO HEALING

The war on sickness may never have been so real for our nation, and our whole world, as it was during the COVID-19 pandemic. While a real sickness, we soon found that this disease was supercharged by the enemy to be not only a tool of sickness, but also one of fear and division. False narratives spread along with the virus, and our freedoms suffered.

I am convinced that this virus was a direct assault on our faith in divine healing, and I think the enemy reveled in getting Christians to move their faith away from a dependable God and towards masks and vaccines that are questionable at best. It was an attack on the Church, the healing promises of God, and the truth of Scripture. Saved and unsaved alike, people got sick and were bound up in fear of this virus, and instead of responding by standing on the Word of God, many forgot His will to heal entirely and turned to the efforts of man to save them.

Satan has stolen health and peace from us long enough, and it's time we took them back. There's no reason for a child of God to live under the same hovering cloud of fear that the world lives under, because as we saw in the previous chapter, it is our God's will to heal us!

When the enemy wears down our faith, it is vital that we understand how to build it back up. We have police officers and people serving in the military in our church, and they understand that when they use their firearms, they must reload to stay in the fight. You can't keep fighting if you don't put more ammunition in, and for the Church our ammunition is the Word of God. The trials of life may have depleted our faith, but our Father wants to rebuild our faith for healing. We must be strengthened in our faith if we are to fight the enemy by rebuking sickness and disease as Jesus did, so it's time to reload on the healing promises of God as we declare war in the spirit on sickness and disease!

God has provided a host of healing promises throughout His Word that will help us rebuild our faith. Remember, faith comes from hearing the Word of God, so we are going to continue looking at Scripture as we examine the pathways God has given us, not just for healing but for many of God's blessings. You see, God's healing power is out there; we've established it's His will to heal. But are you experiencing it? If not, you can learn the key pathways God gives us for receiving healing.

Faith Comes by the Word

Whether you grew up hearing sound biblical teaching about healing or if you were taught all wrong, God has a fresh opportunity for you. If you have an open heart toward the Word, God can plant a message in your spirit so you can receive it afresh, and that is incredibly important if you have had an experience where someone was not healed. Many people have a story of someone who was sick and went to be prayed for at church, or attended an event with a healing evangelist—yet they died, and you're left confused. Why did that person die? Why were they not healed? Did they not have the faith?

I do not claim to have all the answers, but the Bible spells out clear paths that God has given us for healing and other miracles throughout the Scriptures. Most importantly, I learned long ago that I cannot base my outcome, miracle, or answered prayer on someone else's experience. We do not know another's heart, and we do not know someone else's faith. We definitely cannot judge anyone else, and no one's faith was ever built up by someone trying to condemn them for their level of faith.

I heard a pastor friend share his story that I found powerful. A woman in his church, another pastor, was diagnosed with a form of cancer. She was very active in the church, and people prayed for her fervently. They did everything they knew to do, yet she still kept getting worse. Eventually, this pastor sharing the story described a visit with her in the hospital. He prayed in advance, asking God for a word for her, because they had believed, prayed, and fasted for this woman's healing. The Lord told him to ask her what she wanted her outcome to be. When he went into her room, he asked her that very frankly.

"You know, Pastor," she said, "I have to be honest. Just between you and me, the moment I was handed this diagnosis, I felt I was going to die." Ultimately, that is exactly what happened—she passed away.

We can sometimes look at circumstances with other people and base our faith for our own experience on what happened to someone else. However, that is not God's plan for us. You don't know what is in another person's heart, and instead of basing our faith on what we can see in the lives of others, we must instead place our trust in the truth of God's Word. We walk by faith, not by sight, and there is no substitute for reloading our faith with the truths in the Bible. God may never give us answers about why a specific someone was healed or not, but He has given us His Word to guide us. We base our faith upon the timeless, inerrant truth of the Word of God, not our experiences.

I have written a book called *Common Questions about Divine Healing*, which you can find on our website at hankandbrenda.org, and I address some of those questions there. However, I want to give you one answer right now.

If you spend all your time lamenting, "Why, why, why did this happen?" you will talk yourself straight into unbelief. The Holy Spirit can share with us all the knowledge that we need for spiritual growth, but there are some questions He will not answer on this side of eternity.

Job, when questioning God, learned that the clay cannot demand answers from the Potter about why it was made or for what purpose, and God gave Job some pretty blunt answers. It is natural for us to wonder, but if we are hung up on our questions, we are often not going to get the answers we seek. Instead, God has given us other answers—those in His Word—that describe His character and will to heal. These truths do not pass away, and they are not subject to another's experiences.

I am so glad that God is the same yesterday, today, and forever and that His compassion does not fail! His Word is immutable, and in it He declares that He is the Lord who heals us! That is the promise on which we stand, no matter what our eyes see.

Learn the Word

We are going to go through more healing Scriptures as we look at the conditions for receiving healing. However, these do not just apply to healing. They apply to prayer and other areas of our spiritual lives.

The first pathway I want to show you is knowing God's promises. Whether it's because of the lack of teaching or incorrect teaching about healing, many Christians do not know God's healing promises or what the Bible genuinely has to say on the subject.

Hosea 4 spells out the dangers of not knowing God and His Word. *"Hear the word of the Lord, You children of Israel, for the Lord brings a charge against the inhabitants of the land: 'There is no truth or mercy or knowledge of God in the land....' My people are destroyed for lack of knowledge"* (Hosea 4:1,6). It's important to see that God was speaking to the people of Israel, those who should have known Him as His children but did not.

The devil is trying very hard to oppose the knowledge of God, because he knows that if the Church truly understands and applies the Word, we will walk in God's promises. He knows he doesn't stand a chance if we do this, so he opposes it at every opportunity!

I love medical science, and God definitely works through doctors and others. However, as an old country preacher said, God does the healing, and the doctors take the credit! There is no healing without the Healer, regardless of how it manifests.

It is vital that we fight back against the devil, that we stand against his attempts to steal our health and keep us ignorant of the Word. If you want to walk in healing, it's time to turn off the TV and shut down the social media feed. Don't make the doctors on the screen your source of hope for healing; God is our source. The devil is the father of lies, and he twists the truth every chance he gets. If you're not careful, relying on the sources of this world will suck the faith right out of you.

Perhaps never before in history has it been so important to draw our truth from the Bible. Lies and disinformation abound, and the media tries to proclaim darkness as light.

When you focus on something, you become confident in it. All too often, we focus more on the fallible resources of this world than the timeless truths of the Word of God. Go ahead and study nutrition, embrace eating right, and take your vitamins—but don't look to those things as your source. Don't just get confident with nutritional facts; be confident with the facts of the Bible! Know God's promises, and apply them in fervent prayer. We live in a generation where we want to take a pill to magically fix every condition, but our greatest daily need is spiritual nutrition from the Word! Garlic pills aren't the Healer of the Church, God is.

The Word of God is the Sword of the Spirit, and we all need to become experts with the sword. God tells us that his people are destroyed for lack of knowledge, and if we want to live in divine healing, we need to build up our knowledge of the Word and spend more time in the Bible than we do even on good things like nutrition. It's not that the information about health is bad, but when we look to it instead of God first, we position ourselves to miss divine healing and replace it with vitamin C. Just like you need your daily nutritional value of foods, vitamins, and other necessities, your spirit needs a steady supply of the Word of God.

I have found that most Bibles don't have enough space in the margins for all the notes I want to make, so I like to write out important verses on cards. Yes, we have access to all of this on our electronic devices, but with those, as we discussed earlier, come distractions. There are no pop-ups on a note card!

However, if you want to refresh yourself in healing Scriptures, you cannot build yourself up if you do not know what they are! God wants to restore our faith, build it up and strengthen it, but that means you need to participate. We need it in us—to get the Word down inside, where it takes root and grows into a bountiful harvest. We know seed time and harvest is a principle of the Word, so plant the seed of God's promises in your spirit so when you need a harvest of healing you can reap back 100-fold!

Obey the Word

The second pathway I want to show you regarding divine healing is living obediently to the Word of God. All the knowledge in the world will help you very little if you do not apply it and live by it. Jesus cautioned His disciples to not just listen to Him but do what He said, and James puts it so well when he writes, "*But be doers of the word, and not hearers only, deceiving yourselves*" (James 1:22).

This is so important because when we get outside of God, we can get outside of His blessing. It's not because He is up there ready to strike you down the minute you do something wrong, but He built a law into the earth that we reap what we sow. God will not be mocked; we will harvest what we plant, and if that seed is obedience to the Word, we are going to harvest a crop of blessing. When we get out of obedience to Scripture, we can interfere with our blessing. Isaiah 1:19 tells us, "*If you are willing and obedient, you shall eat the good of the land.*"

Let's look back at a Scripture we covered earlier and uncover another aspect of it. Exodus 15:26 tells us, "*If you diligently heed the voice of the Lord your God and do what is right in His sight, give ear to His commandments and keep all His statutes, I will put none of the diseases on you which I have brought on the Egyptians. For I am the Lord who heals you.*" Notice, God lists a number of stipulations before he gets to the promise. Jesus kept the law for us, but we participate as we apply ourselves diligently to learning and applying God's Word.

All of us have sinned and fallen far short of God's glory, but thankfully Jesus paid the price for our failures. The blood of Jesus covers every mess up and does what we could not do, keeping the Law. But we cannot negate and neglect the statutes of Scripture, turning a blind eye or disobedient heart to God's principles. He does not change, and His Word does not change, so if it says it in the Bible, we want to do it! We want to live by it!

The Bible covers aspects of our character a lot and particularly in the New Testament it talks about our attitude. God covers how important it is that we use our tongue to agree with Him, rather than complaining or letting it be empowered by hell itself. God took the time to inspire people to write about our decision-making, our thought processes, and so many other things that touch on every aspect of our daily lives. God has given us His standards, but more than that, an insight into His character. He shows us what He's like, but then He tells us to be like Him. We need to know those Scriptures if we are to walk in obedience with them and be more like our Father, transformed from the inside out by the work of the Holy Spirit. God wants us to partner with Him in obedience, and when we do so, we align ourselves with the Word, and the flow of God's blessings will come to us as a natural result.

The Bible tells us that the way is narrow that leads to life. Jesus is the gateway, the only way that leads to life. Our ministry has been criticized for preaching on righteousness and adhering strictly to God's instructions. However, the Holy Spirit has reminded us that He has established a narrow path, one that leads directly through Jesus. Anyone who tries to come in another way is a thief, and the devil will try to steal your healing and other blessings by advocating other ways that are not God's way. Some people don't like that God seems so restrictive, but He is not trying to ruin your fun. He knows that there's only one way, the way He prescribes within Scripture, and He wants to lead you on that path.

Jesus told His disciples, "*But everyone who hears these sayings of Mine, and does not do them, will be like a foolish man who built his house on the sand*" (Matthew 7:26). The storms are going to come, and when they do, if you have tried to go any other way or built on any other foundation except Jesus Christ, the Word made flesh, then the storms are going to bring it all crashing down. God is a loving Father, and He doesn't want that for you.

God wants you to live and operate in His blessings, including healing, and that means it's not enough to just know the Word—we need to live obediently to it. But how do we know if we're living according to the Word?

Examine Yourself

We have already looked at a few of the pathways toward walking in healing that God has given us—knowing and obeying the Word. When I talk to people, sometimes they ask why God would put conditions on His blessings. I urge them to think of them like this: it's like God showing us the laws of driving. If you don't know and obey the rules of the road, you're going to make mistakes. You might just get a ticket, but you could also be in an accident that could potentially hurt or kill you or others. Wouldn't it be a kindness for someone to teach you the laws of the road before you drive, both to yourself and for those around you?

The next pathway I want to discuss is that of self-examination. When teaching about the Lord's Supper, Paul writes,

> *But let a man examine himself, and so let him eat of the bread and drink of the cup. For he who eats and drinks in an unworthy manner eats and drinks judgment to himself, not discerning the Lord's body. For this reason many are weak and sick among you, and many sleep. For if we would judge ourselves, we would not be judged. But when we are judged, we are chastened by the Lord, that we may not be condemned with the world.*
> 1 Corinthians 11:28-32

This does not mean that you live every day on eggshells, in fear that you will do something that will make you unworthy. Jesus made you worthy, but Paul is writing this to New Testament Christians. In writing about self-examination, Paul describes a work of the Holy Spirit within you that's consistent with David asking the Lord to search his heart and point out any wicked way in him in the Psalms.

We live in what I like to call snowflake culture, where people are afraid to look at themselves critically. They will readily point their fingers at others and get offended, but if you are willing to do the hard work of looking inside and then dealing with whatever the Holy Spirit points out, it is a pathway to God's blessing. The Church, as God's people, needs to take self-examination seriously and hold ourselves accountable for obeying the Word.

Acting on What God Shows You

Dodie Osteen, Joel Osteen's mother, had an interesting life story about when she was healed of cancer. The doctors gave her almost no chance of living, and now the Osteens share a powerful story of how she handled it when they told Dodie she was going to die. Reduced to just skin and bones in her fight against cancer, Dodie took her healing into her own hands. She felt led to make it right with anyone with whom she had a problem. She wrote notes to many different people and sent out cards through the mail asking them to forgive her for anything she may have done. She did this for anyone she could think of, including people she may have lost contact with decades before. Now, this was not the only thing that contributed to her healing, I'm sure, but she felt led to examine herself and deal with any unforgiveness in obedience to God's Word and the prompting of the Holy Spirit. She was mightily healed by the power of God when the doctors said she would not live another year!

We are quick to quote verses such as Mark 11:23-24:

For assuredly, I say to you, whoever says to this mountain, 'Be removed and be cast into the sea,' and does not doubt in his heart, but believes that those things he says will be done, he will have whatever he says. Therefore I say to you, whatever things you ask when you pray, believe that you receive them, and you will have them.

However, all too often people ignore the next two verses:

And whenever you stand praying, if you have anything against anyone, forgive him, that your Father in heaven may also forgive you your trespasses. But if you do not forgive, neither will your Father in heaven forgive your trespasses.

Self-examination and obedience are connected to our healing, because our healing is linked with our forgiveness.

Paul instructs, *"Examine yourselves to see if your faith is genuine. Test yourselves. Surely you know that Jesus Christ is among you; if not, you have failed the test of genuine faith"* (2 Corinthians 13:5 NLT). He is urging us to take a look inside and then accept the correction of the Holy Spirit in any areas that are not pleasing to Him.

I want to remind you, God is not up in heaven picking apart every little thing we do. But He does want us to live within the parameters He gives us, both in the Word but also from that still, small voice of the Spirit within us.

Do you have the Spirit of God living inside of you? Then you have no doubt felt the nudge of the Holy Spirit, at some point or another, telling you to stop doing something or start doing something. He never condemns us, but the Holy Spirit is the One who convicts us of sin. He guides us and teaches us the right way.

He might bring up something with me like, "Brenda, you ought not to talk about that person like that." Or He may correct my words, "Speak life, not death with your words."

The important part is that when God brings something up, we take it to heart, stop whatever it is we are doing, and adjust to God's instructions. Whether it's forgiveness, our words, or something else entirely, it's vital that, like Dodie, we respond with obedience.

When we fail to listen to the correcting voice of God, we can be undoing our prayers for our healing! Just look at how important it is; for example, that husbands treat their wives with honor. We read in 1 Peter 3:7, "*Husbands, likewise, dwell with them with understanding, giving honor to the wife, as to the weaker vessel, and as being heirs together of the grace of life, that your prayers may not be hindered.*" This is so important to God, He gives us a warning—disobedience can hinder our prayers.

God's Word is light and life. We read in Proverbs 4:20-22, "*My child, pay attention to what I say. Listen carefully to my words. Don't lose sight of them. Let them penetrate deep into your heart, for they bring life to those who find them, and healing to their whole body.*" Obeying God's Word, and letting Him search your heart for any areas where you are not obeying, is life and healing for your whole body!

God has truly made a pathway for us to healing, and I cannot emphasize enough how important it is to not just be a hearer of the Word but a *doer*, one who does not shy away from the conviction of the Holy Spirit. If you want to walk in healing, heed God's instructions and take the narrow path that He has laid out for us.

CHAPTER 5

BUILDING FAITH

Faith is a requirement for healing, but I think some people get the wrong idea. You don't go to the gym wondering if you're strong enough to lift 40 pounds. You just go to the gym, and you do your workouts—and in the process, you grow stronger. This is a picture of our faith. When it comes to the natural workout; however, we seem to easily understand where our fitness level is. We also seem to better understand that getting fit is a process that doesn't happen overnight. Rather, it's a lifelong process of growth and development that requires commitment and dedication. When it comes to our faith we sometimes seem to have a harder time accepting this process.

If you feel as though your faith is building for the first time or that it needs to recover from some blows, don't worry about whether or not you have enough faith to be healed. Simply do what God has told you—obey the Word—and let God build you up. You're going to get stronger if you just do it and put in the reps, but the result isn't instantaneous, any more than the results of a natural work-out regimen are instantaneous.

The problem is, as we all know, it takes effort to get out your gym bag and go work out. Most of us don't like working out, but everyone likes the results! I'd much rather sit on the couch with a magazine, but I like feeling stronger and healthier, so I get up and go. If you want your faith to be healthier—and thus your body—you've got to spiritually get up and put in the effort God has prescribed for walking the path of healing. If you don't, you'll never get stronger.

We read this encouragement in Hebrews: *"Therefore, since we are surrounded by such a huge crowd of witnesses to the life of faith, let us strip off every weight that slows us down, especially the sin that so easily trips us up. And let us run with endurance the race God has set before us"* (Hebrews 12:1 NLT). This is why it's not enough to just know the Word; we need to obey it and lay down every weight that so easily ensnares us.

We do things every day that not only fail to build our faith, they actually hold us back. We can choose to build our faith—or we can choose to obsess in fear over the news, social media, or a doctor's report. Don't get caught up worrying if you have enough faith. Stop doing things that tear you down, and start doing things that build you up! As you evaluate your heart, if God shows you anything that is pulling you down, let it go. Instead, do that which pleases God! Don't just walk this pathway of faith—let God build you up to run and finish the race God has set before you!

According to Your Faith

In this chapter, we're going to look at a principle we see in Jesus' ministry. Repeatedly, He told people some variation of this phrase: "let it be done according to your faith." You see, faith can be measured, and not only that, it is by *our* faith that we are healed, which I will show you in the Word shortly.

Now, before we go any further, let me emphasize that we are not to judge other people's faith. Years ago, a man whose wife had died from a serious illness said that if he heard anyone say that she didn't have the faith to be healed—that it was her fault she died because she didn't have the faith—he would want to hurt them! I didn't know his wife at all, but it stuck with me that we cannot assume that someone else does or does not have the faith for healing. A young man, whom a friend of mine knows, has, at least for now, walked away from God. This is partly due to his mother's death from cancer during his teenage years. His church berated her and his family for not having enough faith for her to be healed. That is not what a hurting young teenager needed to hear from his church, and we do not want to be a condemning voice, for there is no condemnation to those who are in Christ. We cannot know another's faith, and it is not our job to judge their faith— that's between them and God.

However, the fact is, God does measure faith. Jesus often commented on people's faith—particularly when the disciples didn't have any! We know faith can be diminished, and we know it can be increased. As we saw earlier, we can build it up with things like the Word, showing that what we feed our faith is even more important than what we feed our physical bodies.

When you understand that, you can build your faith for certain things. Some people have great confidence that God will provide for them financially but not for God to heal, so in a situation like that, you can feed on the healing Scriptures to build your faith as you walk the path to healing God has laid out before you.

Let's look at some examples of faith together. Paul writes of Abraham, a father of our faith, *"God told him, 'I have made you the father of many nations.' This happened because Abraham believed in the God who brings the dead back to life and who creates new things out of nothing"* (Romans 4:17 NLT). Our God calls the things that do not exist yet, like our healing, as though they do!

Paul goes on,

Even when there was no reason for hope, Abraham kept hoping—believing that he would become the father of many nations. For God had said to him, 'That's how many descendants you will have!' And Abraham's faith did not weaken, even though, at about 100 years of age, he figured his body was as good as dead—and so was Sarah's womb.

Romans 4:18-19 NLT

Abraham had a word from God to stand on, and hearing that word built his faith. At the age of 100, as good as dead and Sarah's womb closed, they had no way of getting pregnant from an earthly perspective—yet Abraham's faith did not weaken! It goes on to say, "*Abraham never wavered in believing God's promise. In fact, his faith grew stronger, and in this he brought glory to God. He was fully convinced that God is able to do whatever he promises*" (Romans 4:20-21 NLT).

I want you to see here that Abraham's faith *grew*, telling us our faith can grow stronger, even in the face of adversity. How many times has your faith been tested... and decreased? Sometimes, when we hope for something and don't see it come to pass, we lose heart. Yet, Abraham shows us that a word from the Lord to stand upon has the opposite effect of increasing our faith!

In Matthew, we read a powerful story of a father who had a situation that decreased his faith. This dad comes to Jesus and says, "*Lord, have mercy on my son, for he is an epileptic and suffers severely; for he often falls into the fire and often into the water. So I brought him to Your disciples, but they could not cure him*" (Matthew 17:15-16). He had tried—and nothing happened.

> *Then Jesus answered and said, 'O faithless and perverse generation, how long shall I be with you? How long shall I bear with you? Bring him here to Me.' And Jesus rebuked the demon, and it came out of him; and the child was cured from that very hour.*
> Matthew 17:17-18

Jesus had every expectation that His disciples were able to cast the demon out of the child. He had already given them the power and authority to cast out unclean spirits,

43

and they'd done it before. Yet here they could not; they didn't have the faith yet.

Jesus is so good, because now He takes the time to instruct His disciples about why they didn't have the faith to cast the demon out. We read,

> *Then the disciples came to Jesus privately and said,*
> *'Why could we not cast it out?' So Jesus said to*
> *them, 'Because of your unbelief; for assuredly, I say*
> *to you, if you have faith as a mustard seed, you will*
> *say to this mountain, "Move from here to there,"*
> *and it will move; and nothing will be impossible for*
> *you. However, this kind does not go out except by*
> *prayer and fasting.'*
>
> Matthew 17:19-21

If you look up the word "unbelief" there, it means fearful and faithless, weak faith. They had seen so many people healed, but in this case their faith was weak, and they couldn't cast out the demon because of their unbelief.

When in His hometown, the Bible tells us that they were offended because of Him. "*So they were offended at Him. But Jesus said to them, 'A prophet is not without honor except in his own country and in his own house.' Now He did not do many mighty works there because of their unbelief*" (Matthew 13:57-58). It wasn't Jesus' faith that was in question—it was theirs!

As I mentioned before, there is no point in worrying that you won't have the faith. We must do the work, putting in the time to build our faith just as we would put in the gym time to build up our muscles. And it all begins with trusting Him and letting the Word build us up.

You see, when we develop our faith, the small seed planted within us can grow and mature into great fruit! If you want to be healed, if you want to walk in God's pathway for healing and experiences in your life, it's not enough to keep your faith in seed form. We want to reap a great harvest!

The Fruit of Healing

When Jesus said that we only need faith the size of a mustard seed, He was not advocating that we only need a small amount of faith in life. That would go counter to other things He's said. Jesus wants us to have strong faith.

Jesus was letting us know that even the smallest seed of faith can grow into a bountiful harvest. A mustard seed cannot feed anyone or flavor your sandwich; the plant that grows from it is that which bears the fruit. We may start with very small faith, just a seed, but sown into fertile ground in our hearts, it can take root and grow stronger.

Jesus tells an important parable about seeds planted in different types of soil. On hard soil, the enemy can gobble up the seed that does not take root. The seed that doesn't go deep gets burned away in the scorching heat of the sun and circumstances. The seed that falls among thorns can spring up, but the cares and concerns of this world will choke it out. However, the seed that is planted in good ground will yield a crop that produces a harvest of 30, 60, and even 100-fold the tiny amount of seed planted! This is the harvest we want—the bountiful harvest of healing!

A mustard seed's worth of faith grows into mountain-moving, demon-kicking, affliction-curing faith. We all begin somewhere, but God has us on a path of growth.

Stay Ready

I want to circle back around to the verse in Matthew where Jesus tells His disciples that this kind of demon would not leave except by prayer and fasting. Notice what Jesus did *not* say—"Let's declare a fast!" A lot of times, Church people will go through a crisis and *then* decide to pray and fast, as if the emergency-oriented fast is going to change something in the circumstance.

No, Jesus is saying that there will be times that various things will come against us, individually and as a Church, and we must have dedicated times of prayer and fasting so we are *ready* when the crisis comes, not try to develop faith after the fact. Mountains are coming, and we want to be ready with a full harvest of faith so we can pray and believe that they will be moved from our path!

We come for battle dressed as we are. If the battle comes and you come naked, your shield of faith at home and you can't find your Bible, you're not going to be ready for standing in faith. Instead, Jesus is saying that to face a trial with the faith necessary, we need to *stay* ready. Fasting doesn't change God; it's to change *us*. We want to build the faith we need for whatever we're going to face in advance, to be prepared for whatever the enemy may try. Jesus already paid the price, already paved the way. God isn't changing; He's ready and willing to heal. The question is: when the crisis comes, will we be ready?

God Is Ready and Willing

I want to leave you with a final thought in this chapter. Jesus never put pressure on Himself for people to be healed. He said again and again, "according to *your* faith, be it unto you." It was never a question of *Jesus'* faith—He had it. It was a question of the faith of those asking for healing.

In Matthew 15, we find the story of a Gentile woman who approached Jesus. *"And behold, a woman of Canaan came from that region and cried out to Him, saying, 'Have mercy on me, O Lord, Son of David! My daughter is severely demon-possessed'"* (vs 22). Here's the interesting thing: Jesus didn't even reply to her! Eventually, He told her, *"I was sent only to help God's lost sheep—the people of Israel"* (Matthew 15:24 NLT).

This Gentile woman models persistent faith for us: *"Then she came and worshiped Him, saying, 'Lord, help me!' But He answered and said, 'It is not good to take the children's bread and throw it to the little dogs'"* (Matthew 15:25-26).

How many of us would have gotten discouraged at this point? Understand, at this time, the message of salvation had not yet come to Gentiles; it was for Jews first. But this woman was not to be dissuaded! Listen to this reply: *"And she said, 'Yes, Lord, yet even the little dogs eat the crumbs which fall from their masters' table'"* (Matthew 15:27).

Faith moves Jesus. *"Then Jesus answered and said to her, 'O woman, great is your faith! Let it be to you as you desire.' And her daughter was healed from that very hour"* (Matthew 15:28).

Whose faith moved Jesus? The Gentile woman's! I marvel that it took the faith of those outside of Israel to illustrate to God's people what true faith looks like. Let's look at another profound example.

In Matthew 8, we read the story of a Roman centurion, a leader in the army, whose servant was sick. The man came to Jesus and told him that his servant was sick, and when Jesus said He would come and heal the man, the centurion had the most amazing reply:

> *Lord, I am not worthy that You should come under my roof. But only speak a word, and my servant will be healed. For I also am a man under authority, having soldiers under me. And I say to this one, 'Go,' and he goes; and to another, 'Come,' and he comes; and to my servant, 'Do this,' and he does it.*
> Matthew 8:8-9

This answer amazed Jesus! *"When Jesus heard it, He marveled, and said to those who followed, 'Assuredly, I say to you, I have not found such great faith, not even in Israel!'"* (Matthew 8:10) Then He gives the centurion his marching orders: *"Then Jesus said to the centurion, 'Go your way; and as you have believed, so let it be done for you.' And his servant was healed that same hour"* (Matthew 8:13).

If Jesus is marveling at faith, we should pay attention. This centurion understood the principles of authority, and it created faith in him that Jesus had the authority to do what He said He could do. Do we understand His authority this way?

Over and over, from the woman with the issue of blood to the men who lower their friend from a hole in the ceiling to blind men healed by the side of the road, the faith of those He healed made them well—*their faith*. Not Jesus' faith. He already had it, and *still* has it.

The question we must ask ourselves is, "Do *we* have the faith to be healed?"

"According to your faith, be it unto you," Jesus told so many. So, would He give that reply to you? Would He call you out, with the Gentile woman and the centurion, for your great faith? Or, like the disciples, would He tell you that there's yet work to do?

It is time for the body of Christ to build our faith! The enemy sought to tear it down, using things like the COVID-19 pandemic. But no weapon he formed against us will prosper, and the gates of hell cannot stand against God's Church!

Whether you have much work to do or little, it is time to begin! It's time to head to the Faith Gym and put in the reps, hearing the Word and obeying it, letting God search our hearts, and repenting of anything that holds us back. Do not question whether you'll have the faith to be healed; just do what God has put before you.

Jesus did not comment about His own faith when He healed people; He commented on *theirs*. We will not be healed by the faith of an evangelist or pastor. We need our faith to be strong, growing stronger as we build it with the

Word. Like Abraham, who faced decades of waiting for his miracle, our faith can grow stronger and increase.

The Bible is full of healing promises, but do we have the faith to take hold of them? I believe the time is ripe. The enemy tried to tear down our faith for healing, but Jesus is building it up! If God could heal a man thrown on the bones of the prophet Elijah long after he was dead, what can living vessels full of faith do as we stand in belief, pulling down healing power out of heaven? It's time to walk in the fullness of God's healing power!

In the next chapter, we're going to look at the power of our words and our declarations, because while we build our faith through the Word, we activate it by declaring it. Let's look at that next step in our path to healing together.

CHAPTER 6

THE POWER OF OUR WORDS

In the previous chapter, we saw how important faith is on our path to healing. Without it, it's impossible to please God. We established that faith is like going to the gym—you put in the reps, and you'll get the result. There's no point worrying if you'll have enough faith to be healed. We saw that we must simply do what God has told us to do.

Remember, if you were going to believe God for divine healing, the most important foundation we have is an understanding of God's Word. It is vital that we refresh our souls in the Bible and keep reestablishing the truth that God wants to heal us in our hearts. I don't think there's ever any revelation of Scripture that is one and done; we must go back to the Word as our foundation, because the devil will try to whittle it down.

We also discussed that it is vital we are not just hearers of the Word but doers. Obedience opens doors to God's blessing. We examine ourselves and invite God to search our hearts so that He can point out any areas of our lives where we aren't living according to the Word. As we do these things, they build our faith and take us down God's path of healing.

I want to re-establish that God is never condemning and that our life in Jesus Christ is a journey of growth. Even the great apostle Paul said that he did not consider himself someone who had already apprehended or attained perfection, but he was pressing forward. I know I am certainly growing every day, and I think it is very important that we do not judge others in their faith journey but instead press forward together toward the prize!

It takes effort to get stronger in the gym, and I believe it takes effort to grow in faith. We must participate. Jesus told many people that their faith had made them whole—*their* faith. God's blessings are freely offered, but we have a part to play. If we want the best of God, we must apply ourselves.

Whether it is healing or provision or any other item on our prayer list, we must take a hard look at our words. God has designed tongues as a way of building our faith, but they can also be perhaps the greatest enemy of faith as well. The words we say are powerful. If we want to walk in God's path for our healing, it is vital that we speak the right words—*God's* Word.

The Power of Agreement

When I was younger, I used to say that if circumstances are tough, and you can't muster up the words of faith to speak, at least just hold your peace and be silent. My belief was that it's better to stay silent than speak the wrong thing for sure! And, while this has some merit, the Lord corrected me on this. He told me that if you do this, it will get you nowhere. The devil may still be taking territory while you're saying nothing. In fact, it was this enlightenment from the Holy Spirit that led me to begin writing my series of devotional books of decrees. I wanted people to immediately have something of faith to declare during adversity, when it's the hardest of all to speak right.

I believe our mouths and the words we speak are some of the biggest reasons we do not receive from God. We may pray one thing, but we talk the opposite to our friends. We say one thing in church, but at home it's something else. All it takes is that unexpected bill, someone discouraging us, or our bodies feeling a certain way and suddenly our mouths do not line up with the truths of Scripture.

Speaking words of faith can be one of the most difficult things to do when we are in a battle because our emotions are screaming and our circumstances are demanding. We can feel foolish or in denial to speak words of faith according to the Bible rather than agreeing with our fears or circumstances.

When we were new to the ministry, honestly it looked like things were not going well. My husband, Hank, went to our pastor and told him it felt like we were in a constant tornado. Every once in a while, we would get a little relief, but then it seemed we got sucked back into the whirlwind. It was battle after battle! We could not find lasting relief. Our pastor told us something that stuck with us: it's only one devil, but he will work hard to get you to agree with his storm.

But if we don't agree with him, we're not giving him any authority over our lives.

I believe that our words are the most important effort we can make to build our faith. They can either agree with the Word, or they can agree with our circumstances—and our enemy! There is great power in agreement. Who do you want to line up with? God and His Word, or the enemy and his attack?

The choice is up to you.

Death and Life in Your Words

We can feel ridiculous when speaking God's truth instead of agreeing with our circumstances. Yet, think about this: Jesus said some seemingly crazy things in the face of circumstances. You may remember that while crossing the lake in a storm, Jesus was asleep in the back of the boat. These seasoned, professional fishermen, who knew this lake extremely well, were terrified! They said they were about to perish as they woke Jesus from His nap. And what does He do? Does He see that these professionals are afraid of the storm and get scared too? No! He says, "Peace, be still" to a *storm*! *And it obeyed!* And then Jesus questioned them, *"Why are you so fearful? How is it that you have no faith?"* (Mark 4:40).

Every evidence of circumstances said that storm was something to fear. Yet Jesus questioned why they were so fearful and commented on their lack of faith. His words were full of faith and full of power.

Jesus made a habit out of speaking counter to circumstances. You will remember in the story of Jairus, whose daughter was dying while Jesus healed the woman with the issue of blood, that Jesus told the crowd the little girl was just sleeping. They knew her to be dead, that she had stopped breathing and had no pulse. Yet Jesus said she was only sleeping, because for Him, bringing her back was no harder than rousing her from sleep.

Jesus, instead of letting circumstances dictate what He said, created new realities with His words. He created atmospheres of healing, life, deliverance, and blessing—all with His tongue.

Remember from Genesis that God created everything through His words. He *spoke* it into being. Hebrews tells us that He upholds everything by the word of His power, meaning that there would be nothing without Him! Everything would cease to exist if He did not uphold it.

Now, get this: Humans are the only creation made in God's image, and He gave us the power to create with our words as well. The devil doesn't have that; he can only corrupt and lie.

Proverbs 18:21 tells us, *"Death and life are in the power of the tongue, and those who love it will eat its fruit."* Think about that for a moment; death and life are in *your words.*

James 3 stands out as one of the most profound and impactful passages in the entire Bible, specifically addressing the power and significance of the words we speak. James begins, *"Indeed, we all make many mistakes. For if we could control our tongues, we would be perfect and could also control ourselves in every other way"* (James 3:2 NLT). Read the Bible as the Bible—what does this say? If we could learn to control our tongues, we would be perfect and able to control ourselves in every other way. He likens it to the bit in a horse's mouth or the rudder of a ship, because though they are small, our tongues can steer our lives.

It isn't just about our minds or our wills, learning Scripture and putting it in our hearts. We must speak it out of our mouths! Could it be that the Bible is actually true, and that you could control all of your body with your tongue? Could you speak healing with your mouth, agreeing with the Word and acting as a true child of God, created in His image? Yes, you can!

Before you start agreeing with your next ache, pain, or symptom, consider instead using your words to speak life and healing to your body. Instead of complaining about what ails you, you can say, "Back pain, I bind you in Jesus' name. I speak healing over you! I speak healing to every cell, every fiber, every joint, every organ, from my bones to my blood to my immune system. Every sickness and disease, I bridle you. Body, be healthy and be strong!"

What if those were your words every time you hurt or felt sick?

The Bible tells us that we can control our bodies with our mouths. Do you understand how significant that is? Your healing is largely dependent on the words that come out of you! I'm going to say that again, because I cannot emphasize this enough:

Your healing is largely dependent on the words that come out of you!

So, that is the positive power of the tongue—it can control our whole body, and we can speak health and wholeness to our bodies. Yet now read the other side: "*And the tongue is a fire, a world of iniquity. The tongue is so set among our members that it defiles the whole body, and sets on fire the course of nature; and it is set on fire by hell*" (James 3:6).

Have you ever thought about the casual phrases that we toss around? Someone might say, "That scared me to death!" or "You almost gave me a heart attack!" Our expressions are full of death, not life. We might say, "My allergies always act up this time of year," or, "Whenever it rains my joints hurt." While those things may be true of your circumstances, do you want to use your mouth to agree with all that? Or do you want to agree with what God says in His Word? It takes a conscious effort to watch our tongues and choose to replace even these silly common phrases with words of life.

Let's revisit the specific phrase from James 3, which asserts that the tongue has the power to defile the entire body. That's big! That means that our tongues have the power to speak life and death ... over us! When we speak curses and negatives over ourselves, we are defiling our bodies. We can defile ourselves with sickness by speaking sickness. That is what the Word is telling us!

Our words have creative power, and we attract things to ourselves with our words. Believe me, the devil is happy to take you up on your negative words. So make it hard on him!

The Lord is even more eager for you to come into agreement and decree His Word with Him. I don't know about you, but I want to be on the winning side. My Bible tells me that just as surely as it rains and snows, producing a crop, *"so shall My word be that goes forth from My mouth; it shall not return to Me void, but it shall accomplish what I please, and it shall prosper in the thing for which I sent it"* (Isaiah 55:11). God's Word *will* accomplish *everything* He wants it to and will prosper *everywhere* He sends it. So if we have the Word ever on our lips, rather than using our words to curse or run our bodies down, we are joining with the irresistible power of God!

Tame Your Tongue

James tells us, *"But no man can tame the tongue. It is an unruly evil, full of deadly poison. With it we bless our God and Father, and with it we curse men, who have been made in the similitude of God"* (James 3:8-9). Now, before you go thinking that this means it is an impossible task, remember that verse two told us that if we could control our tongues, we would be perfect and control ourselves in every way. I don't believe that God would put this in the Bible if it were not possible for us, with the help of the Holy Spirit, to do that which is impossible by willpower alone—control our tongues.

Your mouth can defile your whole body, but I believe that God has also intended it to be a weapon that can *purify* our bodies. If we could not do anything to fix it, the Bible would not give us the opportunity. Yet, it says that if we can bridle our mouths, we will control our bodies, and God does not put standards in the Bible when there's no hope we can do it. We simply cannot do it *alone*, apart from God.

God told this to Joshua: *"This Book of the Law shall not depart from your mouth, but you shall meditate in it day and night, that you may observe to do according to all that is written in it. For then you will make your way prosperous, and then you will have good success"* (Joshua 1:8). God is telling us what to do, exactly—to keep the Word in our mouths, instead of cursing.

Kenneth Hagin tells a story about his daughter, Pat, who had a growth on her eye. He was traveling and speaking a lot, and he told his wife that he was just going to listen to what God had to say. He opened his Bible, and he read healing passages over and over. He sought divine guidance on the matter. To strengthen his spirit, he immersed himself in the Scriptures, reinforcing their teachings within his soul. He didn't just read it once or casually; he meditated on it day and night. Keep in mind, he already knew all these Scriptures by heart, but he was reaffirming his faith by reading these verses over and over again, just like we have been discussing in this book. He didn't do anything fancy, he just read the Bible. And one day his wife called to tell him that the growth had simply disappeared!

You have heard the adage, "garbage in, garbage out," and this is especially true for our lives. Put the Word in, and you will change *your* words. Put the garbage of the world in, and you'll get garbage out of your mouth. And if you really want to up your game, *read the Bible out loud*! There is power when you speak the Word where you can hear it—and the devil can hear it too!

Proverbs tells us, *"A wholesome tongue is a tree of life, but perverseness in it breaks the spirit"* (Proverbs 15:4).

That word *wholesome* also means curative or medicinal in the Hebrew—it's saying that a healing tongue is a tree of life. This is obviously significant when we are praying for someone, but always remember you can speak words of healing to *yourself*.

Elsewhere in Proverbs we read, *"There is one who speaks like the piercings of a sword, but the tongue of the wise promotes health"* (Proverbs 12:18). Do you want to pierce yourself or speak words that promote health and healing?

Super Over Natural

The natural order of things is subject to the supernatural. The words that we declare from our mouths can move the natural things. Just look at Jesus in the storm—the supernatural governed the natural, and the storm obeyed the sound of His voice. Sickness fled at His command, and demons were bound by His softest whisper.

Cancer is a perversion of the natural cells in your body. We can speak God's promises and expect the natural order of things to be set by the supernatural order. Just as we can speak the negative and defile our bodies, we can do the opposite and speak health and wholeness over them.

James 3 goes on to caution, *"Out of the same mouth proceed blessing and cursing. My brethren, these things ought not to be so. Does a spring send forth fresh water and bitter from the same opening?"* (James 3:10-11) Surely it is not right for blessings and cursing to pour out of the same mouth! This does not mean just curses as in bad four-letter words. James is talking about cursing ourselves and our bodies with our words.

Now, sometimes we are going to make mistakes. An idle word is going to slip out. So, what do we do? We speak life to build ourselves right back up. Don't condemn or berate yourself; just speak life. Speak the Word. Declare God's promises! This, dear reader, is putting in the effort. Earlier we used the analogy of going to the gym, and this is exactly what it means to put in the reps to build your faith.

I love this Psalm: *"Does anyone want to live a life that is long and prosperous? Then keep your tongue from speaking evil and your lips from telling lies!"* (Psalm 34:12-13 NLT). Do you want life? Do you want health so that you can live a long time and prosper in all of God's blessings? Then watch your tongue and choose to speak life!

The evil this Psalm speaks of, I'd like to point out, means anything that disagrees with God. That means that unbelief is evil. Negativity? Evil. Anything opposed to God's Word is evil, and that includes sickness and disease because God has given us healing promises!

It's tempting to give many things a voice that are not going to bless you. Even something as simple as complaining about having "the Mondays" can be a negative that you just don't need. How much better would it be to speak life over your work week? Don't agree with the grind of the week and the tiredness and how little you like your job; speak by faith that you walk in God's blessing, health, healing, and divine energy. Speak prosperity over the work of your hands and grace and patience for all the stuff life's going to throw at you. This is speaking life, rather than death.

The doctor may tell you that you were going to be on a medicine for the rest of your life, but just because she said it doesn't mean you need to go repeating it to everyone you meet. Don't brag about it or seek pity; oppose that natural prognosis with a supernatural declaration! Instead of repeating that doctor's words to everyone you know, speak life over yourself! Speak life to that condition.

If you have gone up for prayer, remind yourself that healing power has gone into you. Use your mouth to speak about the times you have been blessed, prayed for, and held up before the Lord. Speak of the promises on your life, read the healing Scriptures—out loud! When you take your medicine, pray over it as you do your meals. Speak blessings over it, that it will work with your body and not against it, that it will not cause side effects, and that it will do its intended function. Pray over your body, that its right state of healthiness will take over for that medicine and divine health and healing will make it unnecessary.

Take your healing Scriptures like you would a prescription! Speak them over yourself as faithfully as you would take a medicine, for unlike medications of this world, the blessings of God come with no sorrows added. There are no negative side effects or complications, only the power and effectiveness of the unmatched Word of God!

On your own, without the help of the Holy Spirit, it might be impossible to tame your tongue on pure willpower. However, you are never alone! You have the Helper, the Paraclete, the Spirit of Jesus Christ living within you, and you *can* master your tongue.

This is especially important because we are about to cover one last aspect of the path to healing, the attacks of the enemy. Binding the enemy is also a function of our tongues. It's so important to put the Word of God in our mouths, because when the enemy attacks with infirmity and sickness, we must speak the Word of God and *fight back* with the true weapons of our warfare. We will look at that together in the next chapter now that you have a greater understanding of how to tame your tongue through the power of God's Word!

CHAPTER 7

BIND THE ENEMY

We have followed God's path to healing throughout this book. We saw how important it is to learn the Word of God, obey the Bible, search our hearts, grow our faith, and watch our words. However, there is one last element I want to cover.

As I mentioned earlier in the book, I believe COVID-19 was a direct attack on the Church's faith for healing. I think the enemy whipped up our fears and managed to get much of the Church in a fearful, defensive posture no different than the people of the world, turning to masks and vaccines rather than faith in the Healer. This should not be so! As surely as God made healing provision for His people throughout Scripture, He has it for us today, and we are not subject to the attacks of the enemy. He has *no* authority.

Unless we give it to him by heeding his lies.

Well, I for one do not intend to let the enemy steal, kill, and destroy my health! Will you? Will you sit back and handle things like someone whose only hope is in the medical treatments of this world, or will you believe in faith in the One who took stripes on His back for your healing on the cross?

As with Joshua, I say as for me and my house, we will serve the Lord!

Agreeing with the Enemy

Romans 10:10 says, *"For with the heart one believes unto righteousness, and with the mouth confession is made unto salvation."* The word "salvation" here means *sozo* or *soteria.* If you look at the definition, this word also means "deliverance" and "healing." In other words, we could say that by believing in our hearts, we are made right with God, and by openly declaring our faith, we are *healed* or *delivered.*

We can speak healing into existence over your life, but also consider this—you can speak healing and deliverance from sickness over the works of the enemy.

We like to say that a declaration a day keeps the enemy away!

In the previous chapter, I asked you who you wanted to agree with—God, or your circumstances. But let me break this down even further for you: when you are sick and afflicted by the enemy and he wants you to buy into his lies, what happens when you use your mouth to affirm your symptoms and circumstances? You're using your words to agree with your enemy!

Dear reader, now that you know the importance and power of your words, do you really want to use them to come into agreement with your *enemy?*

When Jesus cast out demons and rebuked the devil, He made declarations—"Devil, come out of him!" It could not be altered after He decreed it. We, too, have the power of declarations in our mouths, and we can speak the Word of God over our sickness and the enemy, full of faith that we are repeating the words of Jesus in the authority of His name.

Are you tired of being sick and tired? Decree your healing and wholeness! Are you tired of being broke? Declare your blessing! Be in obedience to the Word, as we've discussed, and then trust that if God said it and you agree with it, it shall be done!

Instead of walking around, using your words to agree with the enemy trying to oppress you, decree God's Word over your health. Decree it over your aches and pains, over the medicine you take, over the food and supplements you eat. They are blessed!

Be careful with your words, because you can use them to speak life and agree with your Father, or you can use them to speak death and agree with your accuser. Now, let's look at how we fight back against the enemy.

Fight Back!

I am convinced that many of us do not receive everything that God has for us because not all sickness and disease is just physical. And it cannot solely be addressed through medicine, health, and wellness, because it is very much connected to the demonic realm. I am all for eating right, working out, and being healthy, but we can get so caught up in the latest health fad, supplement, or treatment that we ignore the fact we have a very real enemy who seeks to kill, steal, and destroy.

If all were as it should be, we should be able to physically do the right things and get perfect results. But we probably all know someone who has eaten healthy and done all the right things, yet still suffered from ill health and disease. One precious pastor I know was a big advocate of colon cleanses and thought he was doing all the right things for his digestive tract, yet he still died of colon cancer. Why is that?

We can forget that sickness and disease are connected to the demonic, and all the vitamins and best food in the world cannot fix a demon. This is why Jesus did not just heal the sick, He healed people *and* cast out demons! It's not popular right now to say that something might be a work of the enemy, but we cannot ignore the fact that in the Gospels and the Early Church, healing and deliverance went hand in hand. It still does.

Healed and Delivered

There can be no doubt that the enemy's work includes sickness. Over and over in Jesus' ministry, we read that He healed the sick and cast out demons—and often one was related to the other. In Matthew we read this powerful Scripture:

> *And Jesus went about all Galilee, teaching in their synagogues, preaching the gospel of the kingdom, and healing all kinds of sickness and all kinds of disease among the people. Then His fame went throughout all Syria; and they brought to Him all sick people who were afflicted with various diseases and torments, and those who were demon-possessed, epileptics, and paralytics; and He healed them.*
>
> Matthew 4:23-24

A few chapters later we read a similar passage:

> *When evening had come, they brought to Him many who were demon-possessed. And He cast out the spirits with a word, and healed all who were sick, that it might be fulfilled which was spoken by Isaiah the prophet, saying: 'He Himself took our infirmities and bore our sicknesses'*
>
> Matthew 8:16-17

In Luke 4:39 we read that Jesus rebuked the fever on Peter's mother-in-law: "*So He stood over her and rebuked the fever, and it left her. And immediately she arose and*

69

served them." The word for "rebuked" here means he made a charge against it and judged it. Last I heard, fevers themselves don't have ears. So, what was He talking to? The thing behind the scenes causing the fever, the enemy.

One of the clearest examples that casting out a demon resulted in healing comes from Luke 13:11-13, which says,

> *And behold, there was a woman who had a spirit of infirmity eighteen years, and was bent over and could in no way raise herself up. But when Jesus saw her, He called her to Him and said to her, 'Woman, you are loosed from your infirmity.' And He laid His hands on her, and immediately she was made straight, and glorified God.*

A few verses later when addressing the ruler of the Synagogue for criticizing Him for healing on the Sabbath, Jesus says, *"So ought not this woman, being a daughter of Abraham, whom Satan has bound—think of it—for eighteen years, be loosed from this bond on the Sabbath?"* Sometimes when we're praying for someone and it just seems like a mess of symptoms it's a spirit of infirmity, as was afflicting this woman. Yet, as with her, no demon of hell can stand against the power of God!

Don't forget the Gentile woman who approached Jesus for her daughter's sake. We read this earlier, so let's pick the story up partway through as Jesus answers this woman's incredible faith:

*But He answered and said, 'It is not good to take the children's bread and throw it to the little dogs.' And she said, 'Yes, Lord, yet even the little dogs eat the crumbs which fall from their masters' table.' Then Jesus answered and said to her, 'O woman, great is your faith! Let it be to you as you desire.' And her daughter was **healed** from that very hour.*

Matthew 15:26-28, emphasis mine

Clearly, this young girl's condition was related to the work of the enemy and when Jesus set her free, she was healed.

I want you to know that there are times our healing requires binding the enemy. Does that mean there is always a demon attached to sickness or health conditions? No, but underneath it all, God is good, the devil is evil, and sickness is a function of the evil in this world. Sickness doesn't come from God, and the enemy seeks to do whatever he can to keep us from abundant life. He wants to bind us up with sickness and disease, as with the woman with the spirit of infirmity.

At hearing this, some people question me and say something like, "Are you saying my sick child has a demon?" Without getting deep into the theology of what the enemy can do in a Christian household, wouldn't you rather deal with the enemy and get free of sickness than try to pretend it's not there because it makes you uncomfortable?

You cannot counsel everything out of people, or medicate everything or fix it with medical procedures.

Sometimes we must be bold and say, "In the name of Jesus, get off of them!"

Jesus Is Our Model

Jesus modeled for us healing and delivering people afflicted by sickness and disease. And just as all authority in heaven and on earth was given to Him, He gave us the authority of His name. Matthew 10:1 clearly states, *"And when He had called His twelve disciples to Him, He gave them power over unclean spirits, to cast them out, and to heal all kinds of sickness and all kinds of disease."* This is repeated over and over in the Gospels—Jesus commissioning His followers to cast out unclean spirits and heal diseases.

We must understand the authority Jesus has given us. He left us His name, and as the centurion understood the authority he was under and thus Jesus' authority to heal, we too must understand the authority He left us with.

> *For though we walk in the flesh, we do not war according to the flesh. For the weapons of our warfare are not carnal but mighty in God for pulling down strongholds, casting down arguments and every high thing that exalts itself against the knowledge of God, bringing every thought into captivity to the obedience of Christ.*
>
> 2 Corinthians 10:3-5

Norvel Hayes was criticized for "always" casting the devil out. "Well," he answered, "that's because Jesus taught me to cast out devils." His book, *Jesus Taught Me to Cast Out Devils* describes this in detail. Jesus modeled it, healing and setting people free of the enemy, and if we want to walk in God's path for healing, we must walk in Jesus' steps.

Some worry that in this day and age, we might offend people if we bind the enemy off of their lives as we pray for their healing. Well, they can keep their sickness, but for me, I'm going to bind Satan any time he is trying to put sickness and infirmity on me and my loved ones! If you are willing to receive healing, be willing to come against the enemy with the weapons of your warfare!

Win the Battle

The devil is bound in the name of Jesus. We are taking back our *right* to be healed, because Jesus has already won the war against sickness and disease when He died on a cross for our sins and rose again victorious over the enemy. Though we may fight battles in our bodies, we know we have the ultimate victory and are *more* than conquerors. Don't let any lie of Satan convince you otherwise; take those thoughts captive and teach them to obey Christ Jesus!

The devil is a liar, and when he lies to you and tells you that you're never going to get better, that you'll always have this condition, that you're going to die—you tell him that he must bend his knee to the name of Jesus! His is the name that is higher than every name that is named, and as blood-bought children of the living God, we walk in every promise of Scripture. I declare the healing promises over you and that no devil of hell can stand against you when you follow the path of healing God has given to His people!

If you want to win your battle with sickness, follow God's path. Don't perish for lack of knowledge, but instead know the Word and the healing promises of God. Don't just be a hearer only, but instead be a doer and obey the Bible. Search your heart, and ask God to reveal it if there is anything in you that does not please Him. If your faith has been beaten down or decreased, put in the reps to grow it and let it flourish. Don't agree with your enemy, but instead use your words to agree with God and His promises. And if the enemy is at work, bind him and cast him out, commanding the healing promises of God over him and his attempts to inflict you and those you love.

God has given you mighty weapons, weapons that win the war on sickness, and no stronghold of sickness can stand against the power of God!

Now, a final appeal: don't just keep this word to yourself. Pray for those who are sick and set them free from the works of the enemy. Walk in health and wholeness and pray for any afflicted by the devil, setting them free. In doing this, we are truly following in the steps of Jesus and carrying out the mission He left us to be His witnesses to the farthest ends of the earth.

Dear reader, you walk in the power of the Holy Spirit. No sickness or disease can stand against you, but it is up to you to stand up and walk in the path of healing God has provided.

Now, go forward, and walk in the victory Jesus won, for by His stripes *you are healed!*

Healing Scripture List

Old Testament

Exodus 15:26

If you diligently heed the voice of the Lord your God and do what is right in His sight, give ear to His commandments and keep all His statutes, I will put none of the diseases on you which I have brought on the Egyptians. For I am the Lord who heals you.

Exodus 23:25

So you shall serve the Lord your God, and He will bless your bread and your water. And I will take sickness away from the midst of you.

Deuteronomy 7:15

And the Lord will take away from you all sickness, and will afflict you with none of the terrible diseases of Egypt which you have known, but will lay them on all those who hate you.

Psalms 91:10
No evil shall befall you,
nor shall any plague come near your dwelling.

Psalms 91:16
With long life I will satisfy him,
and show him My salvation.

Psalms 103:2-3
Bless the Lord, O my soul,
And forget not all His benefits:
Who forgives all your iniquities,
Who heals all your diseases.

Psalms 105:37
He also brought them out with silver and gold, and there was none feeble among His tribes.

Psalms 107:20
He sent His word and healed them, and delivered them from their destructions.

Proverbs 4:20-22
My son, give attention to my words;
Incline your ear to my sayings.
Do not let them depart from your eyes;
Keep them in the midst of your heart;
For they are life to those who find them,
And health to all their flesh.

Proverbs 16:24
Pleasant words are like a honeycomb,
Sweetness to the soul and health to the bones.

Proverbs 17:22
A merry heart does good, like medicine,
But a broken spirit dries the bones.

Isaiah 32:3
The eyes of those who see will not be dim,
And the ears of those who hear will listen.

Isaiah 35:6
Then the lame shall leap like a deer,
And the tongue of the dumb sing.
For waters shall burst forth in the wilderness,
And streams in the desert.

Isaiah 53:4-5
Surely He has borne our griefs and carried our sorrows; yet
we esteemed Him stricken, smitten by God, and afflicted.
But He was wounded for our transgressions, He was bruised
for our iniquities; the chastisement for our peace was upon
Him, and by His stripes we are healed.

Isaiah 53:10
Yet it pleased the Lord to bruise Him;
He has put Him to grief.
When You make His soul an offering for sin,
He shall see His seed, He shall prolong His days,
And the pleasure of the Lord shall prosper in His hand.

Isaiah 57:19

"I create the fruit of the lips: Peace, peace to him who is far off and to him who is near", Says the Lord, "And I will heal him."

Isaiah 58:8

Then your light shall break forth like the morning,
Your healing shall spring forth speedily,
And your righteousness shall go before you;
The glory of the Lord shall be your rear guard.

Jeremiah 30:17

"For I will restore health to you and heal you of your wounds," says the Lord.

Malachi 4:2

But to you who fear My name the Sun of Righteousness shall arise with healing in His wings; and you shall go out and grow fat like stall-fed calves.

New Testament

Matthew 8:16-17

When evening had come, they brought to Him many who were demon-possessed. And He cast out the spirits with a word, and healed all who were sick, that it might be fulfilled which was spoken by Isaiah the prophet, saying: "He Himself took our infirmities and bore our sicknesses."

Matthew 4:23
And Jesus went about all Galilee, teaching in their synagogues, preaching the gospel of the kingdom, and healing
all kinds of sickness and all kinds of disease among the
people.

Matthew 8:8-9, 13
Lord, I am not worthy that You should come under my roof.
But only speak a word, and my servant will be healed. For
I also am a man under authority, having soldiers under me.
And I say to this one, "Go," and he goes; and to another,
"Come," and he comes; and to my servant, "Do this," and
he does it....

Then Jesus said to the centurion, "Go your way; and
as you have believed, so let it be done for you." And his
servant was healed that same hour.

Mathew 9:12
When Jesus heard that, He said to them, "Those who are
well have no need of a physician, but those who are sick."

Matthew 10:1
And when He had called His twelve disciples to Him, He
gave them power over unclean spirits, to cast them out, and
to heal all kinds of sickness and all kinds of disease.

Matthew 14:35-36
And when the men of that place recognized Him, they sent
out into all that surrounding region, brought to Him all who
were sick, and begged Him that they might only touch the

hem of His garment. And as many as touched it were made perfectly well.

Matthew 15:26-28

But He answered and said, "It is not good to take the children's bread and throw it to the little dogs."

And she said, "Yes, Lord, yet even the little dogs eat the crumbs which fall from their masters' table."

Then Jesus answered and said to her, "O woman, great is your faith! Let it be to you as you desire." And her daughter was healed from that very hour.

Luke 4:18

The Spirit of the Lord is upon Me,
Because He has anointed Me
To preach the gospel to the poor;
He has sent Me to heal the brokenhearted,
To proclaim liberty to the captives
And recovery of sight to the blind,
To set at liberty those who are oppressed.

Luke 9:11

But when the multitudes knew it, they followed Him; and He received them and spoke to them about the kingdom of God, and healed those who had need of healing.

Acts 3:6-9

Then Peter said, "Silver and gold I do not have, but what I do have I give you: In the name of Jesus Christ of Nazareth, rise up and walk." And he took him by the right hand and lifted him up, and immediately his feet and ankle bones received strength. So he, leaping up, stood and walked and entered the temple with them—walking, leaping, and praising God. And all the people saw him walking and praising God.

Acts 9:34
And Peter said to him, "Aeneas, Jesus the Christ heals you. Arise and make your bed." Then he arose immediately.

Romans 8:11
But if the Spirit of Him who raised Jesus from the dead dwells in you, He who raised Christ from the dead will also give life to your mortal bodies through His Spirit who dwells in you.

1 Peter 2:24
Who Himself bore our sins in His own body on the tree, that we, having died to sins, might live for righteousness— by whose stripes you were healed.

3 John 2
Beloved, I pray that you may prosper in all things and be in health, just as your soul prospers.

ABOUT THE AUTHOR

PASTOR BRENDA KUNNEMAN is co-founder of One Voice Ministries and with her husband, Pastor Hank, pastors Lord of Hosts Church, a thriving church in Omaha, Nebraska. She is a captivating preacher with a powerful prophetic anointing who preaches a cutting-edge kingdom message seeing lives changed by specific prophecies for both individuals and churches.

Pastor Brenda ministers at conferences and churches both nationally and internationally, as well as travels and ministers with her husband, flowing together uniquely in prophetic demonstrations of the gifts of the Spirit.

Together, the Kunnemans host their own nationally and internationally televised program, New Level with Hank and Brenda, and have recently launched their own streaming network, OVTV (OneVoiceTV.net) where not only their church services are watched worldwide, but other notable programs as well. As an author, Pastor Brenda has written several books with the newest being prophetic devotionals, The Daily Decree Series.